Games and Activities That Reinforce Listening, Speaking, Reading, and Writing Skills

Written by
Rita Jamieson

Editor: Kim Cernek
Illustrator: Darcy Tom
Cover Illustrator: Reggie Holladay
Designer: Moonhee Pak
Cover Designer: Moonhee Pak
Art Director: Tom Cochrane
Project Director: Carolea Williams

Special thanks to Elizabeth McKibbin and Debbie Smith for their encouragement.

© 2001 Creative Teaching Press, Inc., Huntington Beach, CA 92649
Reproduction of activities in any manner for use in the classroom and not for commercial sale is permissible.
Reproduction of these materials for an entire school or for a school system is strictly prohibited.

TABLE OF CONTENTS

Introduction 4

LISTENING

Bugs in the Box 7
Cookie Counting 8
Shaping up on Colors 9
Directional Dismissal 10
Fast or Slow—How Does It Go? 11
Animal Antics 12
Start Your Engines! 13
Knock, Knock, Tricky Fox 14
Can of Worms 15
Four-Star Band 16
Spider's Subtraction 17
Dinosaur Deals 18
A Lollipop Walk 19
Edible Button Math 20
Pass It On 21

SPEAKING

The Sharing Can 22
The Holidays Are Taking Shape 23
Butterfly Behavior 24
Here's the Scoop! 25
Sharing Shapes and Colors 26
Spinning Sounds 27
Roll-a-Rhyme 28
Shadow Shapes 29
Wonderful Watermelon 30
Don't Look Back! 31
Wallpaper Patterns 32
Who Is That Masked Listener? 33
We're Nuts about Nuts! 34
From Top to Bottom 35

READING

The Cookie Monster 36
Color My Words 37
Silly Simon 38
Free Parking 39
Bugs Beware! 40
The Biggest Fish 41
Hop into Reading 42
Toss Across 43
Cookie Connection 44
What Is in This Muffin Tin? 45
Scrambled Sentences 46
A Picture-Perfect Breakfast 47

WRITING

House Hues 48
Photo Fun 49
Little Bunny You-Hoo 50
Bookworms 51
Funny Bunny Rhymes 52
Building Bingo Boards 53
Picture This! 54
This Is the Place 55
Soup's On! 56
What's in the Box? 57
Two of a Kind, But Not of Like Mind 58
Down by the Park 59
Animal Poetry 60
Birthday Greetings 61

Reproducibles 62

INTRODUCTION

A child's language skills undergo a major "construction period" during the early years of learning. Children develop their listening skills, increase their vocabulary, and begin to make the transition from oral to written language. *Building Better Language Skills* gives you all of the tools and plans you need to provide opportunities for children to build their language skills. This book covers the four areas of language—listening, speaking, reading, and writing—in fun, open-ended ways that are meaningful and relevant to children.

FOUR AREAS OF LANGUAGE

The games and activities in this book give children many opportunities to explore ways of receiving and expressing both oral and written language.

Listening

Children learn to listen to language long before they are able to produce it. The activities in this section promote the development of listening skills as children follow verbal directions and respond through movement and speech to what they hear. Children will also develop other skills, such as color and shape recognition and identification, counting, and problem solving, as they participate in these fascinating, cross-curricular activities that involve active listening.

Speaking

Every early-childhood teacher knows that speaking is one of children's favorite forms of communication! Implement the activities in this section to help children correctly pronounce words, build vocabulary, speak in complete sentences, improve fluency, and develop other oral language skills that will help them become effective speakers.

Reading

Reading is a complicated process that first requires mastery of a series of basic skills. Use the activities in this section to help children recognize and identify letter and word patterns, identify and produce phonemic sounds (phonemic awareness), utilize picture clues, and match phonemic sounds to the letters of the alphabet that represent them (phonics). Children will love these inviting, hands-on activities that promote successful reading.

Writing

Reading and writing go hand in hand. As children develop the skills they need to decode printed words, they become interested in encoding in written language their own thoughts and ideas. The activities in this section allow for every level of writing ability in your class—from scribbling to drawing to printing the alphabet. Encourage children to record information and give directions through written language as they participate in the shared-writing activities.

Choose from 55 phonemic awareness, phonics, math, shape and color, movement, and critical-thinking games and activities that encourage children to follow directions, use simple sentences in sequential order, identify and generate rhymes, respond to oral and written language, discriminate sounds, problem-solve, and more. These cross-curricular activities and extension ideas also teach children to retain, recall, and share information; expand their knowledge of language; and increase their enjoyment of learning new concepts.

Copy on card stock several sets of the reproducible letter cards (pages 65–67), number cards (pages 68–69), and picture cards (pages 82–85). Cut apart the cards, laminate them, and keep them handy for use in many of the games and activities in this book.

Building Better Language Skills will help you provide early-childhood and English-as-a-second-language children with authentic, significant experiences that balance their interests and needs. The activities are easy to implement and feature fun, flexible, and concrete experiences that will help children build a strong foundation for language development.

BUGS IN THE BOX

Make several copies of the Bugs reproducible, color the bugs, and cut apart the cards. (Or, use a bag of plastic bugs.) Number the boxes from 1 to 10. Place the boxes in random order on a flat surface, and ask a small group of children to arrange them in numerical order. Set a container of the paper bugs or plastic bugs beside the boxes. Point to a box and say *How many bugs belong in this box?* Invite a child to place into the box the number of bugs that matches the number on the box. Repeat the process with another child until all of the boxes have been filled. Then, replace the bugs in the container, and repeat the activity with a different group of children.

Materials

- ✓ Bugs reproducible (page 62) or plastic bugs
- ✓ crayons or markers
- ✓ scissors
- ✓ 10 small boxes without lids
- ✓ container

Concepts

- Following directions
- Number recognition
- Numerical order
- Counting

Extensions

- Encourage children to give each other the directions in the activity.
- Read aloud one of David A. Carter's bug books before you begin the activity. Then, invite children to use construction paper and art supplies to make their own bugs to place in the boxes.

Listening

COOKIE COUNTING

Materials
- Cookies reproducible (page 63)
- card stock
- crayons or markers
- scissors
- dried black beans
- glue
- paper plates

Concepts
- Following directions
- Counting
- Addition

Extensions
- Place at a learning center a set of cookie cutouts with one to six beans glued on separate ones, and invite children to find two cookies that create a sum you name. For example, children could pick up the cookies with three and five beans to make the sum eight.
- Read aloud *The Doorbell Rang* by Pat Hutchins (Greenwillow). Combine several sets of cookie cutouts, and use them to demonstrate how the cookies are divided in the story.

Give each child a card-stock copy of the Cookies reproducible, and ask children to color and cut out their cookies. Give each child 21 black beans. Ask children to glue one bean on the first cookie, two beans on the second cookie, and so forth. Divide the class into pairs, and give them simple directions to follow, such as *Find a cookie that has two "raisins" on it* or *Find a cookie that shows your age*. Or, invite pairs of children to give each other directions, such as *Find two cookies that have five "chocolate chips" together*. After the activity, invite children to glue their cookies to a paper plate and then take home their goodies to "share."

8 Listening

SHAPING UP ON COLORS

Cut out two circles, one from red construction paper and one from blue. Repeat to make two squares. Then, cut out two rectangles, one from yellow construction paper and one from green. Repeat to make two triangles. Laminate the eight shapes, and place them in a paper lunch sack. Give each child a Shapes in Our World reproducible. Choose a shape from the sack (e.g., a yellow rectangle), and ask children to identify the shape and color. Say *Find something that is the shape of a **rectangle** on your paper and color it **yellow.*** Choose a new shape from the sack, change the boldfaced words to the new shape and color, and repeat the process until children have colored most of the shapes on their paper. Invite children to take their paper home and describe the shapes and colors to their family members.

Materials

- Shapes in Our World reproducible (page 64)
- scissors
- red, blue, yellow, and green construction paper
- paper lunch sack
- crayons or markers

Concepts

- Following directions
- Shape identification
- Color identification
- Matching

Extensions

- Place five or six different-colored shape cutouts in the top row of a pocket chart, and have children name the shapes and the shapes' colors in order from left to right. Change the order of the shapes, and repeat the activity.
- Ask children to draw their family interacting at the park on the Shapes in Our World reproducible. Have children write a story about their picture on the back of their paper.

Listening

DIRECTIONAL DISMISSAL

Materials
- letter cards (pages 65–67) and/or number cards (pages 68–69)

Concepts
- Following directions
- Critical thinking
- Letter recognition
- Number recognition

Extensions
- Point to an object in the classroom. To dismiss children, have them name words that rhyme or words that begin or end with the same sound as the object.
- Place a small, shallow box near the door. Each time the class leaves the room, announce a different way for them to move past the box. For example, say *Walk around the box as you leave the room* or *Jump over the box before you go out the door.*

Use this activity to dismiss children for recess or lunch. Invite children to leave when they hear a direction that applies to them. For example, say *If you have brown hair, you may go outside* or *If your name begins with /s/, you may go to lunch*. Or, give each child a letter or number card. Announce a letter or number, and ask the child who holds the matching card to hand it to you before he or she is dismissed.

10   Listening

FAST OR SLOW— HOW DOES IT GO?

 Make an enlarged copy of the Fast or Slow Picture Cards, and color and cut apart the cards. Ask children to name things that are fast or slow. Invite children to stand in a circle, display the cards one at a time, and describe the picture on each card. Ask them to clap slowly when they see something that goes slowly and clap fast when they see something that goes fast. Invite children to stand along one side of the room. Display and describe a card, and ask children to walk slowly to the other side of the room if the picture shows something that goes slowly and walk fast if the picture shows something that goes fast. Repeat the activity with the rest of the cards.

Materials

- ✓ Fast or Slow Picture Cards (page 70)
- ✓ crayons or markers
- ✓ scissors

Concepts

- Following directions
- Critical thinking
- Movement

Extensions

- Read aloud a version of *The Tortoise and the Hare*. Discuss with children the benefits of going slowly and taking your time.
- Invite children to name other opposites, such as hot and cold, wet and dry, or bumpy and smooth, and ask them to draw pictures for these pairs of opposites.

Listening 11

Materials

✓ Animal Picture Cards (page 71)
✓ crayons or markers
✓ scissors
✓ containers
✓ music/CD or cassette player

Concepts

- Following directions
- Music
- Movement
- Critical thinking

Extensions

- Place number cards in the containers. When a child draws a card, ask him or her to clap that number of times, and encourage the class to count the number of claps they hear.
- Place letter cards in the containers. When a child draws a card, ask him or her to say a word that begins with the sound that letter makes, and invite the class to name the letter.

ANIMAL ANTICS

Arrange chairs back-to-back in two lines, one for each child. Make three or four copies of the Animal Picture Cards, color them, and cut them apart. Place each set of cards in a separate container, and set the containers on separate chairs. Invite each child to stand beside a separate chair. Play music, and ask children to stop beside the closest chair when they hear the music stop. Stop the music, and have the children who are standing beside chairs with a container draw a card and take turns imitating the movement and sounds of the animal on their card. Challenge the class to identify the names of the animals. Collect the children's cards, and set the containers on different chairs. Play the music again, and repeat the activity until there are no cards left in the containers.

12 Listening

START YOUR ENGINES!

Make a class set and an enlarged copy of the poem "Stoplight," and display the enlarged copy on a chart stand. Give each child three small paper plates; green, yellow, and red paint; and a paintbrush. Have children paint one red, one yellow, and one green. As the paint dries, read aloud "Stoplight," and invite the class to join you as you read it again. Give each child a copy of the poem and a large sheet of black construction paper. Have children glue the poem to their paper. Tell children to glue the red, yellow, and green plates in order lengthwise on the other side of their paper. Invite children to take home their "stoplight" and read aloud the poem with family members.

Materials

- ✓ "Stoplight" poem (page 72)
- ✓ chart stand
- ✓ small paper plates
- ✓ green, yellow, and red paint
- ✓ paintbrushes
- ✓ large sheets of black construction paper
- ✓ glue

Concepts

- Following directions
- Art
- Choral reading

Extensions

- Encourage children to memorize the poem "Stoplight" and create movements to demonstrate the words.
- Play a game of Red Light, Green Light with the class.

Green means that it's time to go.

Listening 13

Materials

✓ basket or bucket
✓ assorted colors of laminated paper ovals or plastic eggs

Concepts

- Color recognition
- Movement
- Counting

Extensions

- Write a number or a letter on separate laminated paper ovals. Repeat the activity, but have the fox call out a number or letter instead of a color.
- Change the character and props to reflect other themes, such as a leprechaun and shamrocks for St. Patrick's Day or a squirrel and nuts for autumn.

KNOCK, KNOCK, TRICKY FOX

 Invite children to sit along one side of a playing area, and ask one child to hold a basket or bucket and stand in the center to play the "fox." Give each child, except for the fox, a laminated paper oval or plastic egg. Teach children to say

Fox: *Knock! Knock!* (pretends to knock on the door)

Class: *What do you want, tricky fox?*

Fox: *Colored eggs.*

Class: *What color?*

Fox: (names a color)

Invite children who have that color egg to stand up and run across the playing area. Tell the fox to collect the eggs from any of the children he or she tags. Have the class repeat the process with new colors until all of the children have run across the room. Invite the class to help the fox count the number of eggs he or she collected. Gather all of the eggs, and choose a different child to play the fox. Redistribute the eggs, and repeat the activity.

CAN OF WORMS

Make several copies of the Worms reproducible, and cut out the worms. Write *Can of Worms* on a strip of paper, and tape it to a container. Write directions, such as *Wiggle like a worm* or *Turn around two times*, on separate worms. Place the worms in the container, and invite children to sit in a circle. Teach them to say *How should we move on this wiggly, giggly day? / Listen very carefully to what the worm will say.* Draw a worm from the can, and shake it so that it appears to wiggle. Read the direction, and invite the class to follow it. Repeat the activity with the rest of the worms.

Materials

- ✓ Worms reproducible (page 73)
- ✓ scissors
- ✓ paper strip
- ✓ tape
- ✓ container

Concepts

- Following directions
- Movement

Extensions

- Give each child a worm to color. Announce a color, and have children who hold that color worm wiggle to the center of the circle and drop their worm into a container.
- Give children a wiggly gelatin treat after the activity in celebration of squiggly worms!

Listening 15

Materials

- ✓ hole punch
- ✓ laminated star cutouts (4 different colors)
- ✓ yarn
- ✓ simple instruments (e.g., drums, rhythm sticks, bells, recorders)

Concepts

- Following directions
- Color identification
- Music
- Movement
- Oral language

Extensions

- Change the boldfaced words in the chant to *rainbow*, and invite the whole class to march and play their instruments together.
- Play "Color Me My World" from *Painting My World* by John Archambault and David Plummer (Youngheart Music) or "Rainbow of Colors" from *We All Live Together* by Greg and Steve (Youngheart Music). Invite children to play their instrument when they hear the color of their star in the song.

FOUR-STAR BAND

Hole-punch a laminated star cutout, insert a piece of yarn through the hole, and tie the ends of the yarn together to make a necklace for each child to wear. Give all children wearing the same color star the same simple instrument to play (e.g., children with red stars all play tambourines), and teach them to chant

Red stars, **red** stars,
Play a tune.
Now go march around the room.

Red stars, **red** stars,
Now slow down.
Take a seat without a frown.

Have children with a red star follow the directions in the chant. Change the boldfaced words to a new color, and repeat the activity.

16 Listening

SPIDER'S SUBTRACTION

Materials
- ✓ Web reproducible (page 74)
- ✓ raisins

Give each child a Web reproducible and five raisins. Teach children to chant

A spider looked at its web and said,
*"There are **5** tasty flies in that sticky thread.*
I will eat just one for my lunch.
*Now there are **4** flies for me to munch."*

Invite children to remove one raisin from the web and eat it after they say the second line of the chant. Ask children to change the boldfaced numbers in the verse, and repeat the activity with the rest of the raisins.

Concepts
- Following directions
- Counting
- Oral language
- Subtraction

Extensions
- Create a maze by using liquid correction fluid to cover some of the lines on the Web reproducible. Draw a bug outside the maze. Ask children to help the spider get to the bug on a revised copy of the reproducible. Ask children to draw the spider's path out of the maze to capture its prey.
- Read aloud a spider story. Give children a Web reproducible, and have them cut out the spider. Invite children to use their spider cutout to retell the story.

Listening 17

DINOSAUR DEALS

Materials
- Dinosaur reproducible (page 75)
- dry erase marker
- assorted coins (pennies, nickels, dimes, quarters)
- resealable plastic bags

Concepts
- Following directions
- Oral language
- Money
- Counting
- Addition

Extension
- Give children unmarked dinosaur papers and a cup of dinosaur crackers. Ask them to place five crackers on their dinosaur, and teach them to say

    I was sitting in the park, eating a snack,
    When a dino came along and fiercely yelled "Attack!"
    I covered my eyes—too afraid to look.
    But one little cracker is all he took!

    Tell children to eat one cracker. Invite children to count how many crackers are left, and have them repeat the activity with the remaining crackers.

Copy and laminate the Dinosaur reproducible for each child in the class. Use a dry erase marker to write a monetary amount (e.g., 6¢ or 42¢) on each dinosaur. Place coins in a resealable plastic bag for each child. Give each child a laminated dinosaur and a bag of coins. Teach children to say

I rode a bus to the nearest toy store
To buy myself a dinosaur.
The salesperson smiled and asked of me,
"Do you have enough money?"

Invite children to place on their dinosaur the number of coins that matches the amount written on the dinosaur. Check children's work, and ask them to return their coins to their bag. Have children exchange their papers, and repeat the activity.

A Lollipop Walk

Materials
- scissors
- construction paper (assorted colors)
- glue
- craft sticks
- lollipops (optional)

 Cut out pairs of circles from assorted colors of construction paper. Glue a craft stick between each pair of circles to create a "lollipop" for each child. Invite children to stand in a circle, and give a lollipop to each child. Stand in the middle of the circle, and have children walk clockwise as you say

I'm so hungry for a treat—
Something sticky, something sweet.
Good golly, please stop!
May I have your lollipop?

Have the class answer *Yes! What color?* Name a color, and invite the children with that color lollipop to walk to the middle of the circle and hand their lollipop to you. Repeat the activity with new colors. As an option, reward children for their skills with a lollipop treat.

Concepts
- Following directions
- Color identification
- Movement
- Matching

Extensions
- Divide the class into two groups. Ask children in the first group to find a child in the second group who has a matching lollipop.
- Instead of circles, use oval cutouts to create an "ice-cream treat" for each child. Change the last two lines of the chant to *Light and fluffy like a dream. / Will you share your ice cream?*, and repeat the activity.

Listening 19

Materials

- ✓ Coat reproducible (page 76)
- ✓ crayons or markers
- ✓ cups
- ✓ O-shaped cereal

Concepts

- Following directions
- Counting
- Subtraction

Extensions

- Have children place cereal buttons one at a time on their copy of the Coat reproducible. Teach children to say *It's cold outside, so I'd better button up. / How many buttons are left in the cup?* After children add each button to their coat, encourage them to count the number of cereal pieces left in their cups.
- Read aloud *Mouse Counting* by Ellen Stoll Walsh (Harcourt Brace). Give children ten cheese crackers. Have them eat one each time a mouse in the story is placed in the jar and count the number of crackers that remain.

EDIBLE BUTTON MATH

Give each child a Coat reproducible to color and a cup of cereal. Invite children to place a piece of cereal on each of the five buttons on the coat. Say **Five** *little buttons as round as can be. / One popped off! Now how many do you see?* Ask children to remove one of the cereal buttons and eat it. Have children count the number of buttons that remain. Change the boldfaced word in the couplet to reflect the new number of buttons, and repeat the activity.

20   Listening

PASS IT ON

Materials
- ✓ number cards (pages 68–69)
- ✓ scissors
- ✓ paper lunch sack
- ✓ soft ball

Copy and cut apart a set of number cards, and place them in a paper lunch sack. Invite children to stand in a circle. Invite one child to draw a card from the sack and announce it to the class. Give a different child in the circle a soft ball, and ask him or her to kick it to another child in the circle. Tell children to continue kicking the ball to each other for the number of times announced. Invite a different child to draw a new number card, and repeat the activity.

Concepts
- Following directions
- Number identification
- Counting
- Movement

Extensions
- Carefully pin a letter card to each child's shirt, and name a word that can be spelled with the letters. Give the ball to the child wearing the first letter of the word, and have him or her kick it to the child wearing the next letter in the word. Have children continue until they spell the word. Announce a new word, and repeat the activity.
- Carefully pin a number card (0–10) to each child's shirt. Give the ball to a child, and say *How many more do you need to make 10?* Have the child kick the ball to a child wearing the number that combines with his or hers to make 10.

Listening 21

Materials

- Sharing Can Parent Letter (page 77)
- hole punch
- ribbon or yarn
- bucket
- construction paper
- clear contact paper

Concepts

- Following directions
- Critical thinking
- Problem solving
- Descriptive language
- Oral language

Extensions

- Change the name on the can to *Thinking Can*, and insert riddles or simple problems for children to solve (e.g., *How many days until Friday?* or *What is the opposite of up?*).
- Change the name on the can to *Can-Do Can*, and insert questions that ask children to demonstrate things they can do (e.g., *Can you tie your shoe?* or *Can you walk like a crab?*).

THE SHARING CAN

Laminate a copy of the parent letter, hole-punch a corner, and use a piece of ribbon or yarn to attach it to the handle of a bucket. Write *Sharing Can* on a piece of construction paper, and use clear contact paper to attach it to the bucket. Invite a child to take home the bucket and place a special item, such as a seashell collection or small toy, inside it. Explain to the child that he or she should ask someone at home to help him or her write three clues about the item (e.g., *It comes from the ocean*) and place the list in the bucket. The next day, help the child read his or her clues to the class. Prompt the class to ask questions about the item or items (e.g., *Can you eat it?*) if they cannot guess what it is from the original clues. When the class correctly names the item, invite the child to remove it from the bucket and pass it around. Send the bucket home with a different child, and repeat the activity.

Speaking

THE HOLIDAYS ARE TAKING SHAPE

Materials
- Holiday Picture Cards (page 78)
- crayons or markers
- scissors
- construction paper (assorted colors)
- pocket chart

Copy, color, and cut apart the Holiday Picture Cards. Cut a large circle, square, and triangle from three different colors of construction paper, laminate them, and place them in the top row of a pocket chart. Show children a picture card, and invite them to name what holiday it represents and why. Tell children you will hide the picture card behind a shape in the pocket chart. Have children close their eyes, and slip the picture card behind one of the shapes. Ask children to open their eyes and guess which shape the card is behind. Repeat the activity with a new picture card.

Concepts
- Following directions
- Descriptive language
- Shape recognition
- Color recognition
- Critical thinking

Extensions
- Place a child's class picture behind a shape. Insert the child's name into the frame *1, 2, peekaboo! Lori, Lori, where are you?*, and invite the class to guess which shape their classmate's picture is behind.
- Choose three picture cards, such as the pumpkin, the heart, and the firecracker. Write the letters *p*, *h*, and *f* on separate shapes, and slip the pumpkin behind the shape marked *p*. Say *pumpkin*, and prompt children to use the first sound in the word to help them find where the picture is hidden. Repeat the activity with the two remaining picture cards.

Speaking

Materials

none

Concepts

- Following directions
- Movement
- Descriptive language
- Cooperation

Extensions

- Choose a new animal (e.g., bullfrog or monkey), and change the action and body parts to relate to that animal. For example, children could chant *Bullfrog, bullfrog, jump through the windows. / Use your strong green legs* or *Monkey, monkey, climb through the windows. / Use your long brown arms.*
- Read aloud *An Invitation to the Butterfly Ball* by Jane Yolen (Boyds Mills). Invite children to imitate the animals in the book.

BUTTERFLY BEHAVIOR

 Invite children to stand in a circle and hold hands. Choose three or four children to be "butterflies," and have them stand inside the circle. Ask the rest of the children to raise up their joined hands. Have the butterflies flap their arms and move in and out of the spaces between the children holding hands as the class chants

Butterfly, butterfly, fly through the windows.
Butterfly, butterfly, fly through the windows.
Butterfly, butterfly, fly through the windows.
Use your colorful wings.

Choose different children to be the butterflies, and repeat the activity.

Speaking

HERE'S THE SCOOP!

Cut out four triangles from brown construction paper, number them 1–4 as shown, and laminate them. Cut out ten circles from assorted colors of construction paper, and laminate them. Attach a piece of magnetic tape to each cutout. Invite children to help you arrange the triangles in numerical order along the bottom of a magnetic surface, and scatter the circles around the triangles. Teach children to chant

I scream. You scream.
We all scream for ice cream.
One scoop, two scoops, three scoops, four.
Keep on scooping more, more, more!

Invite individual children to place the matching number of "scoops" on each triangle to create "ice-cream cones." After children fill each cone, return the circles to the bottom of the board, and invite other children to repeat the activity.

Materials

- ✓ scissors
- ✓ construction paper (assorted colors)
- ✓ magnetic tape
- ✓ magnetic board or cookie sheet

Concepts

- Following directions
- Numerical order
- Counting

Extensions

- Add more triangles and circles to the board to encourage children to count quantities larger than four. Or, use only two or three colors of circles, and invite children to make patterns with the scoops on "plain cones."
- Make four copies of the Bowl reproducible (page 88), cut out each bowl, and glue a picture card (pages 82–85) to each bowl. Write the letters that spell the name of each picture on separate circles. Invite children to assemble the circles along the top of the bowls to spell the corresponding words.

Speaking

SHARING SHAPES AND COLORS

Materials
- scissors
- red, yellow, and blue fabric
- glue gun or needle and thread
- funnel
- rice or dried beans

Concepts
- Shape identification
- Color identification
- Critical thinking

Extensions
- Place a red, a blue, and a yellow container in the middle of the circle. Give each beanbag to a child, and give each child a direction to follow, such as *Drop the yellow beanbag into the red box.*
- Make a beanbag for each pair of children to share. Invite children to form two lines, and have each child face his or her partner. Give children directions to follow, such as *If you have a blue beanbag, toss it to your partner* or *If you have a red beanbag, hop it over to your partner.*

Cut two circles from red fabric, two triangles from yellow fabric, and two squares from blue fabric. Use a glue gun or a needle and thread to join the matching shapes together along the edges, leaving a small opening. Use a funnel to fill the beanbags with rice or dried beans, then close the openings. Invite the class to sit in a circle. Hold up the red beanbag, and say

Look at this shape.
What could it be?
(Children answer *circle.*)
Look at the color.
Name it for me.
(Children answer *red.*)

Pass the beanbag around the circle. Teach children to say *Pass the beanbag very slow. / Tell us a **red** thing that you know.* Ask the child who is holding the beanbag when the chant ends to name something that is red. Or, change the boldfaced word to *circular*, and invite the child to name something that has the shape of a circle. Use the yellow triangle and the blue square to repeat the activity.

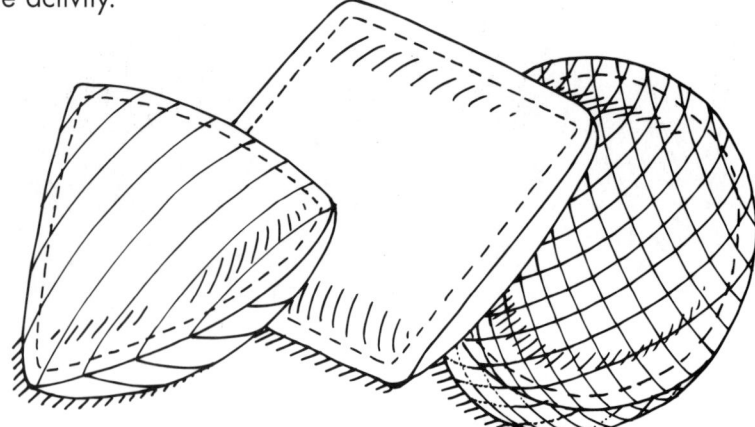

26 Speaking

SPINNING SOUNDS

Materials
- letter cards (pages 65–67)
- scissors
- tape
- lazy Susan

Copy and cut apart a set of letter cards, and tape four or five of them to the top of a lazy Susan. Invite the same number of children as letter cards on the wheel to sit in a circle, and place the lazy Susan in the center. Invite a child to spin the wheel, announce the letter that stops before him or her, and name words that begin with the same sound as the letter. Repeat the activity with new letter cards or a different group of children.

Concepts
- Following directions
- Letter recognition
- Phonemic awareness
- Phonics

Extensions
- Give each child an index card with a rime (e.g., *-it* or *-op*) written on it. Invite children to spin the wheel and add the sound of the letter to their rime to make a word.
- Instead of letter cards, tape pictures of animals or objects to the lazy Susan. Invite children to spin the wheel and describe the shape, size, color, and other physical characteristics of the picture that stops before them.

Speaking

ROLL-A-RHYME

Materials
- Nursery Rhyme Picture Cards (page 79)
- crayons or markers
- scissors
- square tissue or gift box
- butcher or construction paper
- tape
- glue

Concepts
- Critical thinking
- Cooperation

Extensions
- Instead of a nursery rhyme, write a category, such as pets, fruit, or colors, on each side of the die. Invite a child to roll the die, and ask each child in a small group to name something that fits into that category.
- Instead of a nursery rhyme, draw a shape, a quantity of dots, or a number on each side of the die, and have children announce the shape or the number that appears on top.

Copy, color, and cut apart the Nursery Rhyme Picture Cards. Cover a square tissue or gift box with paper. Glue a picture card on each side of the box to create a "die." Invite a small group of children to take turns rolling the die, and have them recite the nursery rhyme that matches the picture on top. Repeat the activity until each group has had a turn.

28 Speaking

SHADOW SHAPES

Invite children to help you choose small items to tape onto a large sheet of blue or black construction paper. Set the paper outside in the sun or near a sunny window for a few hours or until the color on the paper fades. Then, remove the items from the paper, and place them in a small container. Tape the paper to a board or wall, and invite children to describe what they see. Ask children to describe the shapes of the shadows and guess which item each shadow represents. Then, place the container of items and the paper at a learning center, and invite children to match the items to the shadows.

Materials

- small items (e.g., keys, paper clips, teaspoons)
- tape
- large sheets of blue or black construction paper
- small container

Concepts

- Observation
- Descriptive language
- Critical thinking

Extensions

- Place magnetic letters on the paper, and repeat the activity. Ask children to identify the letters, produce the sounds they make, and name words that begin and end with those sounds.
- Invite children to use small objects you supply or those they bring from home to make their own "shadow collages." Ask them to describe their collages to each other.

Speaking

WONDERFUL WATERMELON

Materials
- scissors
- paper plates
- red and green paint
- paintbrushes
- watermelon cut into slices
- glue

Concepts
- Art
- Counting

Extensions
- Begin counting aloud, and invite children to line up in numerical order according to the number of seeds on their slice of watermelon.
- Divide the class into small groups, and encourage them to create math problems based on their watermelon seeds, such as *Five seeds plus three seeds equals eight seeds.* Encourage older children to write the number sentences for their problems.

 Cut several paper plates into triangles, and give each child a triangle, red and green paint, and a paintbrush. Ask children to paint one edge of their triangle green and the rest of it red to resemble a slice of watermelon. Give each child a slice of watermelon. Have children save their seeds after they eat their fruit, and teach them the following verse sung to the tune of "Row, Row, Row Your Boat":

We love watermelon
Juicy and so sweet.
Cut one open.
Count the seeds.
It's our favorite treat!

Ask children to count the number of seeds from their slice of watermelon and glue them to their painted triangle once the paint is dry. Invite children to exchange triangles and count a classmate's seeds.

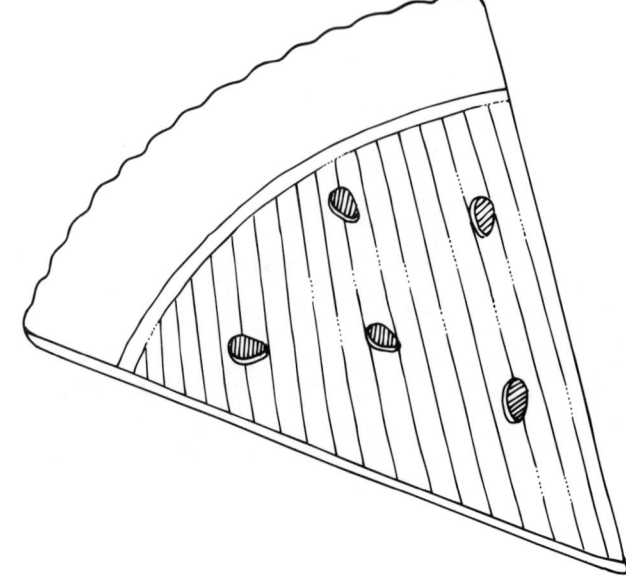

DON'T LOOK BACK

 Place an animal sticker on the back of each child's shirt. Invite children to walk around the room and ask each other yes or no questions about their sticker, such as *Does my animal swim?* or *Is my animal green?* After children correctly identify their animal, give them their sticker to place on their hand, and ask them to sit in a circle. Ask children questions about their animals, such as *Whose animal has four legs?* or *Whose animal lives on a farm?*, and invite them to stand when their animal is described.

Materials
✓ animal stickers

Concepts
- Cooperation
- Social interaction
- Critical thinking
- Classification

Extensions
- Invite children to imitate the movements and sounds of the animal on their sticker.
- Invite children to draw the habitat of their animal (e.g., a swamp for a crocodile or a tree for a bird) and place their sticker in their picture. Ask children to describe their picture to the class.

Speaking

WALLPAPER PATTERNS

Materials
- scissors
- wallpaper samples
- glue
- 3" (7.5 cm) construction paper squares

Concepts
- Cooperation
- Matching
- Color identification
- Pattern identification
- Descriptive language

Extensions
- Tape several wallpaper squares to a chalkboard, and ask children to help you name the pattern on each square, such as dots, squiggly lines, or purple flowers. Invite children to "read" the pattern sentence from left to right. Change the order of the squares, and repeat the activity.
- Invite children to cut out their own shapes and figures from wallpaper samples. Ask them to glue their shapes to a piece of paper and describe their picture to the class.

Cut two 3" squares from eight different wallpaper patterns to make 16 squares. Glue each wallpaper square to a construction paper square, and place these "pattern cards" with the wallpaper side facedown in a grid on a flat surface. Invite three or four children to sit around the grid, and have them take turns turning over cards until they find a match. Ask children to describe the colors and patterns on their matching squares. Repeat the activity with a different group of children.

WHO IS THAT MASKED LISTENER?

Copy, color, and cut out the Mask reproducible. Laminate the mask, and tape it to a paint-stirring stick or ruler. Invite children to sit in a circle. Ask a volunteer to stand in the middle and hold the mask in front of his or her face. Point to a child in the circle, have that child stand in front of the "Masked Listener," and prompt the child to say *Hello, Masked Listener! How are you today?* Encourage the "Masked Listener" to guess who is talking. If the "Masked Listener" cannot guess the voice, invite children to give clues about the mystery child, such as *He is a boy* or *Elephants are her favorite animal.* After the "Masked Listener" correctly names the other child, have him or her give that child the mask, and repeat the activity.

Materials

- ✓ Mask reproducible (page 80)
- ✓ crayons or markers
- ✓ scissors
- ✓ tape
- ✓ paint-stirring stick or ruler

Concept

- Problem solving

Extensions

- Give children paper plates and art supplies, and invite them to make a mask that resembles themselves for use in the activity.
- Place three objects, such as a ball, a book, and a shoe, in the center of the circle. Invite a child to cover his or her face with the mask. Remove an object, and then ask the child to take off the mask and guess what was removed.

Speaking 33

Materials

✓ containers of assorted nuts and seeds
✓ paper plates

Concepts

- Following directions
- Classification
- Cooperation
- Critical thinking

Extensions

- Invite the class to join you as you read aloud *Peanut Butter and Jelly* by Nadine Bernard Westcott (Dutton Children's Books). Serve peanut butter and jelly on crackers to celebrate how much fun nuts can be!
- Instead of nuts, invite the class to sort shells. Change the first line of the chant to *We have special shells* and the announcement to *"Spe-shell" delivery!*, and repeat the activity.

WE'RE NUTS ABOUT NUTS!

 Divide the class into two groups, and give each group a container of assorted nuts and seeds and several paper plates. Invite the groups to sort the nuts and seeds by shape, color, and/or texture. Ask each group to place nuts and seeds with the same characteristics (e.g., brown, small) on a plate. Have both groups chant

We're nuts about nuts.
How about you?
Can you tell what's the same
About these few?

Have the groups exchange one of their plates and announce *Nutty delivery!* Give each group a few minutes to examine the nuts and seeds they received, and invite them to explain why the nuts and seeds have been sorted in that way. Have the groups return the plates, and invite them to repeat the activity with another type of nut and/or seed.

34 Speaking

FROM TOP TO BOTTOM

Materials

- ✓ *Tops and Bottoms* by Janet Stevens (Harcourt Brace)
- ✓ Vegetable Picture Cards (page 81)
- ✓ crayons or markers
- ✓ scissors
- ✓ chart paper
- ✓ tape

Make an enlarged copy of the Vegetable Picture Cards, and then color and cut apart the cards. Read aloud *Tops and Bottoms*. Encourage children to name vegetables from the story that grow either above or below the ground. Draw a horizontal line across the middle of a piece of chart paper, and write *above* at the top of the paper and *below* at the bottom. Hold up the corn picture card, and say **Corn** *is a vegetable that I know. / Where in my garden does it grow?* Invite a child to tape the card either above or below the line on the chart paper. Choose a new picture card, change the boldfaced word in the couplet, and repeat the activity with a different child.

Concepts

- Directional words
- Critical thinking

Extensions

- Find pictures of animals that hibernate for the winter, such as bears and snakes. Repeat the activity, but have children decide which animals hibernate above or below ground.
- Copy and cut apart the Animal Picture Cards (page 71). Change the words on the chart paper to *land* and *water*, and ask children to decide where each animal lives.

Speaking 35

Materials

- Cookies reproducible (page 63)
- scissors
- magnetic tape
- 2 cookie sheets
- large sheet of construction paper
- tape

Concepts

- Following directions
- Letter recognition
- Phonemic awareness
- Phonics

Extensions

- Prepare a set of cookies that are different colors. Invite children to feed the cookie monster the color or amount of cookies that you name.
- Read aloud *The Chocolate Chippo Hippo* by Vincent Andriani (Scholastic) or *If You Give a Mouse a Cookie* by Laura Joffe Numeroff (HarperCollins) as children enjoy a cookie snack.

THE COOKIE MONSTER

Make five copies of the Cookies reproducible, and write each letter of the alphabet on a separate cookie. Cut out and laminate the cookies. Attach a piece of magnetic tape to each cookie, and scatter the cookies on a cookie sheet. Cut a head from construction paper, draw facial features on it, and tape it to the top edge of a separate cookie sheet. Cut out paper arms and legs, and tape them to the sides and bottom of the cookie sheet. Invite individual children to "feed" the cookie monster the first letter of their name. To extend learning, name a type of cookie (e.g., chocolate chip, sugar, peanut butter) or ingredients that are used to make cookies (e.g., flour, butter, eggs), and have children feed the letter or letters that make the first sound of each word to the cookie monster.

36 Reading

COLOR MY WORDS

Cover a large container with dark-colored contact paper. Attach uniform pieces of red, yellow, blue, and green tape to the rim of the container to divide it into four equal parts. Use a permanent marker to write *red* on three red plastic clothespins, and place them inside the container. Repeat the process with three yellow, three blue, and three green clothespins (twelve total), and place the clothespins inside the container. Invite a small group of children to sit around the container. Have children take turns drawing a clothespin from the container, reading the color word, and attaching it to the matching section of the rim. Place the clothespins back in the container, and repeat the activity with a different group of children.

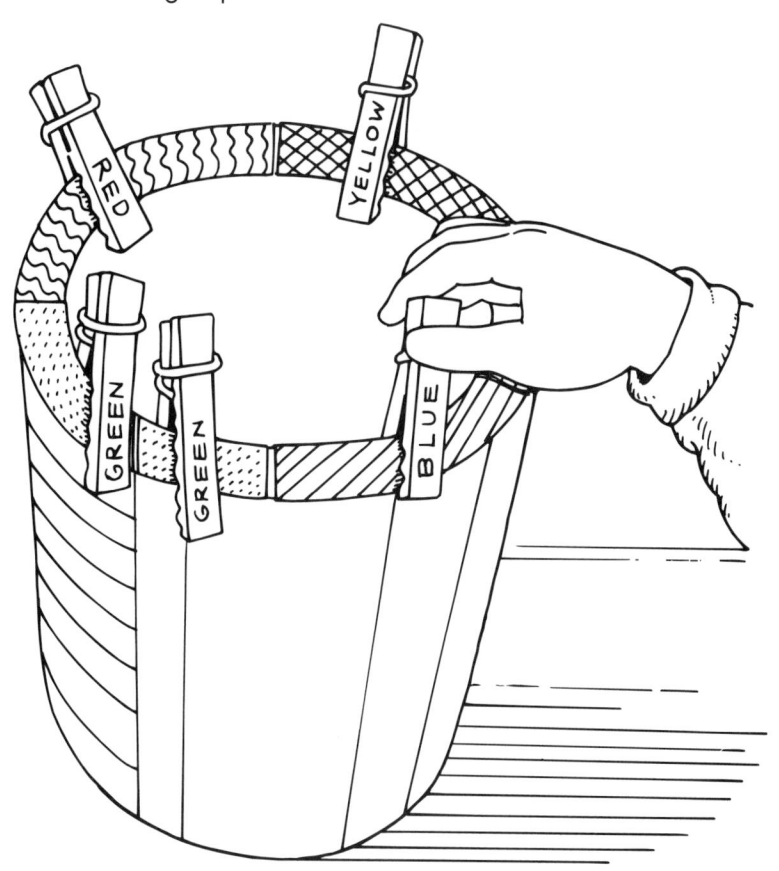

Materials

- ✓ large container (e.g., oatmeal canister or coffee can)
- ✓ dark-colored contact paper
- ✓ red, yellow, blue, and green colored tape
- ✓ permanent marker
- ✓ red, yellow, blue, and green plastic clothespins

Concepts

- Color identification
- Word recognition
- Matching
- Cooperation
- Oral language

Extensions

- Cover several containers with contact paper, and tape a picture card (see pages 82–85) to each container. Write the letters that spell the name of each picture on separate clothespins, and place them inside the matching container. Invite children to clip the clothespins to the rim in the correct order to spell the word.
- Clip a colored clothespin to each shirt of twelve children. Invite children who do not have a clothespin to arrange their classmates to create a colored pattern.

Reading 37

Silly Simon

Materials
- ✓ glue
- ✓ star cutout
- ✓ paper strip
- ✓ stapler

Concepts
- Following directions
- Oral language
- Phonemic awareness
- Critical thinking

Extensions
- Change Silly Simon's directions in the activity to *Touch something on your body that rhymes with ___*. For example, the child wearing the crown could say *Touch something on your body that rhymes with* hose.
- Have Silly Simon point to a child and use that child's name in the frame *Michelle, touch something in the room that starts with /r/*.

Glue a star cutout to the top of a strip of paper, and staple together the ends of the strip to create a crown. Invite children to stand in a circle, and invite one child to stand in the middle and wear the crown. Prompt the child to say *Silly Simon says, "Touch something on your body that starts with /t/."* Have children touch a part of their body that starts with /t/, such as toes or tummy. Ask Silly Simon to change the sound, and then choose another child to wear the crown and repeat the activity.

Touch something on your body that starts with /l/.

38 Reading

FREE PARKING

Copy and cut apart a set of ten picture cards. Cut off the tops of ten cartons, cover them with contact paper, and tape a picture card to the front of each carton. Write the letter that matches the first letter of each picture card on a separate white label. Place each label on a separate toy car. Invite a child to "park" each car in the "garage" with the matching picture card. Invite a different child to repeat the activity.

Materials

- picture cards (pages 82–85)
- scissors
- 10 empty quart-size milk or orange juice cartons
- contact paper
- tape
- white labels
- small toy cars

Concepts

- Letter recognition
- Phonemic awareness
- Phonics
- Critical thinking

Extensions

- Cover ten cartons with contact paper, and place one colored dot-sticker on the first carton, two stickers on the second one, and so on. Number white labels from 1 to 10, and place them on ten separate toy cars. Invite children to park each numbered car in the garage with the matching number of dots.
- Tape five picture cards to separate cartons. Write a rhyming word for each picture on a separate white label, and place the labels on separate toy cars. Invite children to park each word car in the garage with the matching picture card.

Reading 39

BUGS BEWARE!

Materials
- Bugs reproducible (page 62)
- crayons or markers
- tape
- flyswatter

Concepts
- Critical thinking
- Oral language
- Descriptive language
- Phonemic awareness

Extensions
- Invite children to help you count the number of legs on each bug from the reproducible. Write these numbers on separate labels, and place the labels beside the corresponding bugs on the paper. Say *These little critters are as leggy as can be. / Swat one with six legs on its body*, and invite a child to swat a bug with the correct number of legs. Change the number, choose a different child, and repeat the activity.
- Choose a book about bugs to read aloud. Invite the class to help you spread peanut butter on celery sticks and then add a few raisin "ants" to their "log." Invite children to eat their snack as you read about some interesting insects.

Make an enlarged copy of the Bugs reproducible, color it, laminate it, and tape it to a board or wall. Ask children to name the bugs on the paper and describe each one. Invite a child to stand beside the bug paper and hold a flyswatter. Say *These little bugs are as buggy as can be. / Swat one that starts with /s/ for me!* Have the class help the volunteer, if necessary. Invite a different child to hold the flyswatter, choose a new sound, and repeat the activity.

Swat one that starts with /f/ for me!

40 Reading

THE BIGGEST FISH

Make a copy of the Fish reproducible, and write *big*, *bigger*, and *biggest* on the corresponding fish. Give each child a large sheet of blue construction paper and the revised reproducible, and ask children to color and cut out their fish. Have them glue their fish in order from smallest to largest on their paper. Ask children to read the words on their fish as they work. Challenge them to find the root word *big* on each fish, and introduce how the suffixes *-er* and *-est* change the meaning of the words. To extend learning, write other size words (e.g., *small, smaller, smallest* or *long, longer, longest*) on the fish for children to read and arrange in order by size.

Materials
- Fish reproducible (page 86)
- large sheets of blue construction paper
- crayons or markers
- scissors
- glue

Concepts
- Size relationships
- Sight words
- Root words
- Prefixes and suffixes

Extensions
- Make several copies of the Fish reproducible, cut out the fish, and insert a brass fastener in the place of the eye on each one. Create a "fishing pole" for each child by tying one end of a string around a magnet and the other around a dowel. Scatter the fish cutouts on the floor, and encourage children to "catch" the fish and arrange them in order by size. Tell children to use a ruler to measure their fish and to return to the "pond" any fish that are not a length specified by you.
- Use a dry erase marker to write a letter or number on each fish cutout. Challenge children to arrange the fish cutouts in alphabetical or numerical order.

Reading 41

Hop into Reading

Materials
- ✓ Frog reproducible (page 87)
- ✓ scissors
- ✓ large sheets of green construction paper
- ✓ dry erase marker
- ✓ crayons or markers
- ✓ glue
- ✓ paper strips
- ✓ stapler
- ✓ tape (optional)

Concepts
- Following directions
- Letter recognition
- Phonemic awareness
- Phonics
- Movement

Extensions
- Use a dry erase marker to label laminated lily pads from 0 to 9, and arrange them as they would appear on a telephone (i.e., three rows of three numbers with 0 in the fourth row). Ask individual children to jump from number to number as they say their phone number.
- Invite children to wear their frog hats as they recite the popular verse "Five Green and Speckled Frogs" or listen to one of the Froggy tales written by Jonathan London (Viking Children's Books).

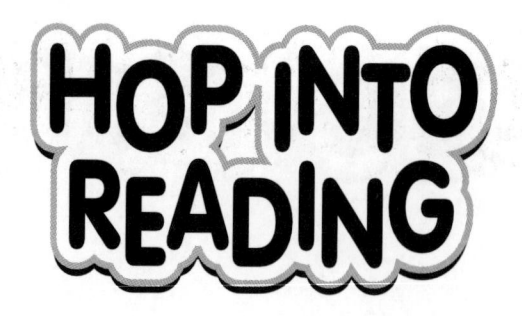

Cut out lily pads from large sheets of green construction paper, and laminate them. Use a dry erase marker to write a letter on each lily pad. (Be sure that the first letter of each child's name appears on a lily pad.) Give each child a Frog reproducible. Help children write their name on their frog and then color it and cut it out. Show children how to glue their frog to a paper strip, staple the ends together to create a crown, and place it on their head. Scatter the lily pads around the room (tape them to the floor if possible), and invite the class to stand in a group along one side of the room. Invite a few children at a time to "hop" to the lily pad with the first letter of their first name. Repeat the activity with children's last names, or invite children to hop onto any lily pad and then name a word or two that begins with that letter.

TOSS ACROSS

Write nine different consonants on separate paper plates, and tape them on the floor in three rows of three. Ask a small group of children to read aloud the letters. Invite children to take turns tossing a beanbag onto one of the plates and naming a word that begins with that letter. Or, announce a word, and ask children to throw a beanbag onto the plate with the letter that begins the word. Repeat the activity with a new group of children, or change the letters on the plates, and repeat the activity with the same group of children.

Lemon starts with l.

Materials

- ✓ paper plates
- ✓ tape
- ✓ beanbag

Concepts

- Following directions
- Letter recognition
- Phonemic awareness
- Phonics

Extensions

- Write words instead of consonants on the plates, and repeat the activity.
- Label the plates from 0 to 9, and invite two children to throw beanbags onto separate plates. Challenge them to add together their numbers and announce the sum.

Reading 43

COOKIE CONNECTION

Materials
- Cookies reproducible (page 63)
- crayons or markers
- scissors
- dry erase marker
- poster board
- chart stand
- tape

Concepts
- Word recognition
- Rhyming words
- Cooperation
- Critical thinking

Extension
- Tape four blank cookie cutouts to the cookie jar, and invite the class to play a few rounds of "Who Stole the Cookies from the Cookie Jar?" Arrange children in a circle, and ask them to close their eyes. Tap four children on the shoulder, and motion for them to take a cookie from the jar and hide it behind their back. Invite children to use the chant to discover who stole the cookies.

Make two copies of the Cookies reproducible, color and cut out the cookies, and laminate them. Use a dry erase marker to write the following words on separate cookies: *bar, car, far, tar, star, bat, cap, fan, stir,* and *tap*. Draw a large jar on a piece of poster board, label it *Cookie Jar*, and laminate it. Display the poster board on a chart stand, and tell children that only cookies with words that rhyme with *jar* can go into the cookie jar. Select a cookie cutout, show it to the class, and use the word written on it in the frame *Should we put **car** in the cookie jar?* Invite children to raise their thumbs in the air if the word rhymes with *jar*, and tape the cutout to the poster board. Repeat the activity with a new cutout (e.g., *Should we put **fan** in the cookie jar?*).

44 Reading

What Is In This Muffin Tin?

Write *b, d, k, m, p,* and *t* on separate white labels, and place one label in each cup of a muffin tin. Set on a flat surface the muffin tin and a container of small items that begin with the letters on the labels. Invite a small group of children to sort the items into the tin according to the first letter of the name of each item. Then, have children name the items they placed in each cup. Place the items back in the container, and invite another small group of children to repeat the activity.

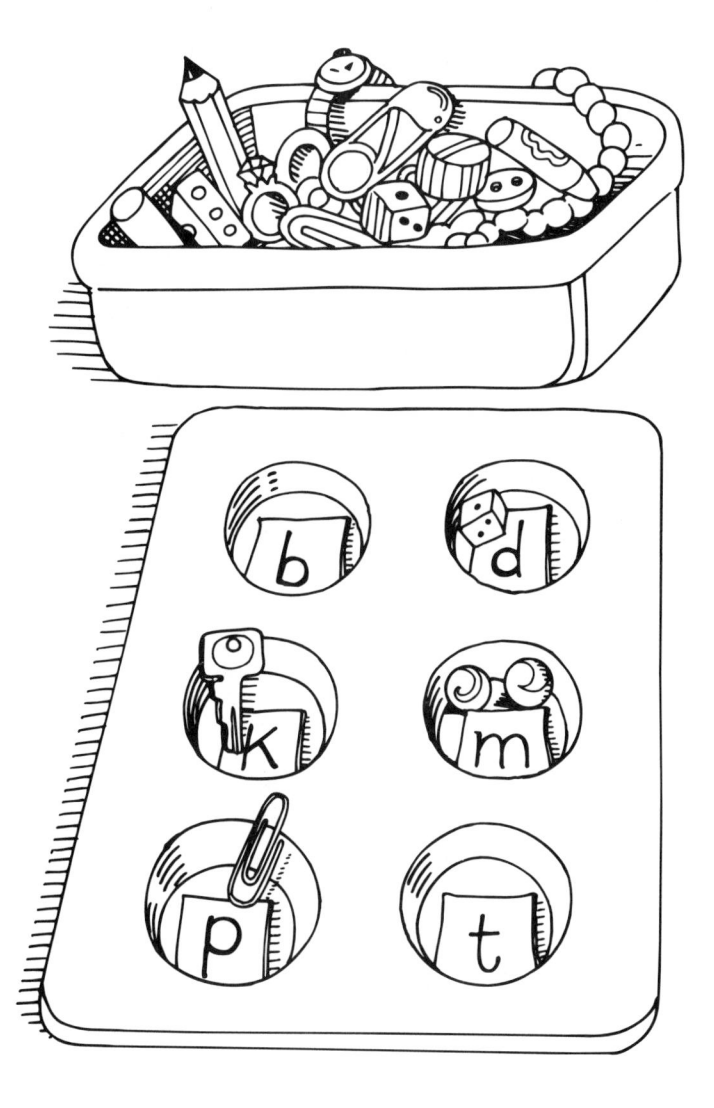

Materials

- white labels
- six-cup muffin tin
- container of small items (e.g., pennies, buttons, safety pins, paper clips, peanuts, dice, marbles, beads, keys, toothpicks)

Concepts

- Letter recognition
- Phonemic awareness
- Phonics
- Classification

Extensions

- Invite children to sort the items according to other characteristics, such as size, color, and texture.
- Number white labels from 1 to 6, and place one label in each cup of a muffin tin. Invite children to place the matching number of pennies or other small items into each cup.

Reading 45

SCRAMBLED SENTENCES

Materials
- index cards
- plastic eggs (2 colors)
- empty egg carton

Concepts
- Following directions
- Cooperation
- Word recognition
- Sentence construction
- Oral reading

Extensions
- Use a dry erase marker to number plastic eggs from 1 to 12, and place them at random in an empty egg carton. Invite a pair of children to place the eggs in numerical order in the carton.
- Read aloud *A Dozen Dozens* by Harriet Ziefert (Penguin Putnam), and discuss with children what a dozen means. Write directions that involve the number 12, such as *Hop up and down twelve times* or *Clap a dozen times*, on index card halves, and place them in a carton. Invite volunteers to choose an egg, and help them read aloud the directions for the class to follow.

Write each word of a six-word sentence, such as *We are going to the zoo*, on a separate index card. Repeat the process with a corresponding sentence, such as *We will see many new animals*. Place the word cards for the first sentence in six separate eggs of one color and the word cards for the second sentence in six separate eggs of another color. Place the eggs at random in an empty egg carton, and invite a pair of children to separate the eggs into two groups. Encourage children to work together to open the eggs of one color and "unscramble" the sentence by arranging the words in order. Ask them to repeat the process with the second set of eggs and then read aloud the sentences to you. Replace the word cards in the eggs, and invite another pair of children to repeat the activity.

46 Reading

A Picture-Perfect Breakfast

Make several copies of the Bowl reproducible, and laminate them. Copy and cut apart several sets of picture cards, and glue them to separate snack-size cereal boxes. Write the word for each picture card on the back or bottom of the box to help children check their work. Divide the class into pairs, and give each pair a laminated bowl, a cup of alphabet cereal, and a few cereal boxes. Invite children to use the alphabet cereal to spell the word for each picture card in their bowl. Have children check their work by matching each set of letters in their bowl to those written on the matching box. Encourage children to repeat the activity with other cereal boxes.

Materials

- ✓ Bowl reproducible (page 88)
- ✓ picture cards (pages 82–85)
- ✓ scissors
- ✓ glue
- ✓ snack-size cereal boxes
- ✓ cups
- ✓ alphabet cereal

Concepts

- Phonics
- Spelling
- Sight words

Extension

- Give children a copy of the Bowl reproducible and a cup of cereal. Invite children to place ten pieces of cereal on their bowl. Say *Ten pieces of cereal. Yummy, yummy, yummy! Give **two** pieces to your hungry, hungry tummy.* Invite children to eat two pieces of cereal and count how many pieces are left in their bowl. Change the first boldfaced word to the remaining number of cereal pieces and the second boldfaced word to another number, and repeat the activity.

Reading 47

HOUSE HUES

Materials
- House reproducible (page 89)
- Mouse reproducible (page 90)
- construction paper
- highlighter
- scissors
- glue
- crayons or markers

Concepts
- Color identification
- Letter formation
- Word formation
- Word recognition

Extension
- Copy and cut out the Mouse reproducible. Make five copies of the House reproducible, and color them five different colors. Cut out the houses, and place them in the top row of a pocket chart. Secretly slip the mouse cutout behind one of the houses. Invite the class to chant *Mouse, mouse, are you in the blue house?* Invite a child to remove the blue house from the chart to see if the mouse is there. Have children repeat the chant with new color words until they locate the mouse.

Give each child a House and a Mouse reproducible and a piece of construction paper. Invite each child to name a color. Use a highlighter to write the color on the roof of the house, and have children trace over the letters. Tell children to cut out their house and glue the roof only to their piece of construction paper. Have children color their mouse the same color as the word they wrote on their house, cut out the mouse, and glue it beneath their house. Display children's papers on a board or wall under the title *What Color Mouse Lives in Your House?* Invite children to read the color word on each house and then lift up the house to see if the color of the mouse matches the word.

48 Writing

PHOTO FUN

In advance, invite children to bring from home photographs of themselves doing something (e.g., baking cookies or doing a somersault). Help each child tape his or her photograph to the top of a piece of paper. Write on the chalkboard the sentence frames (<u>Name of child</u>) is special. (He/She) can _____. Invite children to complete the sentences with their name and a few words that describe what they are doing in their photograph. Have children write their sentences below their photograph. Invite emergent writers to dictate the sentences to you, and encourage experienced writers to copy the sentence starters from the board and use invented spelling to complete their sentences. Ask children to read their sentences to each other.

Materials

- ✓ photographs
- ✓ tape
- ✓ paper

Concepts

- Sentence formation
- Letter formation
- Word formation
- Spelling
- Oral reading

Extensions

- Invite individual children to say *This is photo fun!* and then something that describes what they are doing in their photograph into a tape recorder. Display children's photographs in a learning center, and place near the photographs a tape recorder, headphones, and the tape of children's voices. Challenge children to match the pictures to the voices they hear.

- Read lines from popular fairy tales and other stories, such as "Not by the hair on my chinny, chin, chin" from *The Three Little Pigs* or "On Wednesday he ate through three plums, but he was still hungry" from *The Very Hungry Caterpillar* by Eric Carle (Philomel). Invite children to identify the stories that match the excerpts.

Writing

Materials

- ✓ Bunny reproducible (page 91)
- ✓ crayons or markers
- ✓ scissors
- ✓ tape
- ✓ paint-stirring stick or ruler
- ✓ chart paper

Concepts

- Oral language
- Phonemic awareness
- Rhyming words
- Word patterns
- Spelling

Extension

- Use the bunny puppet to point to an object in the classroom, and change the last two lines of the verse to *He hopped on a table / And said, "This starts with /t/."* Give the puppet to a child, and invite him or her to repeat the activity.

LITTLE BUNNY YOU-HOO

Copy, color, and cut out the Bunny reproducible. Laminate the bunny cutout, and tape it to a paint-stirring stick or ruler to create a bunny puppet. Chant

Little Bunny You-Hoo,
Hopping through the classroom,
*Hopped on a **book***
*And said, "This rhymes with **hook**."*

Write *book* and *hook* on a piece of chart paper. As you write the words, emphasize that they have the same spelling pattern (*-ook*). Ask children to name other words with the same spelling pattern, and write them on the chart paper. Use these words to replace the second boldfaced word in the verse, and invite the class to chant with you. Or, change both boldfaced words in the verse to new rhyming words, and repeat the activity.

50 Writing

BOOKWORMS

Make several copies of the Worms reproducible, and cut out the worms. Write on separate worms sentences from stories that children know well, such as "Yellow duck, yellow duck / What do you see?" from *Brown Bear, Brown Bear* by Bill Martin Jr. and Eric Carle (Henry Holt and Company) or "Goodnight kittens / Goodnight mittens" from *Goodnight Moon* by Margaret Wise Brown (HarperCollins). Find an old, discarded book, use an exacto blade to cut out a large square from the middle pages to create a hollow space, and place the worm cutouts inside. Invite each child to pull out a worm from the book, and help children read aloud the sentence on their worm. Give each child a piece of drawing paper. Ask children to draw a picture about the story and dictate to you or write the title of the story at the top of their paper. Display children's work around the room, and invite the class to match the worms to the corresponding stories.

Materials

- Worms reproducible (page 73)
- scissors
- old, discarded book
- exacto blade
- drawing paper
- crayons or markers

Concepts

- Literature appreciation
- Oral reading
- Letter formation
- Word formation
- Art

Extensions

- Use the names of characters from familiar stories in the activity.
- Write unique vocabulary words from popular books on separate worms, and invite children to name the story in which those words appear.

Writing 51

Funny Bunny Rhymes

Materials
- ✓ Bunny reproducible (page 91)
- ✓ picture cards (pages 82–85)
- ✓ crayons or markers
- ✓ scissors
- ✓ tape
- ✓ paint-stirring stick or ruler
- ✓ chart paper
- ✓ colored markers

Concepts
- Rhyming words
- Letter formation
- Word patterns
- Spelling
- Choral reading

Extension
- Have children use the bunny puppet to retell a Max and Ruby story by Rosemary Wells (Dial Books) or a Davy tale by Brigitte Weninger (North-South Books).

Copy, color, and cut out the Bunny reproducible. Laminate the bunny cutout, and tape it to a paint-stirring stick or a ruler to create a bunny puppet. Copy and cut apart a set of picture cards, and place them near a piece of chart paper. Ask a child to hold up the bunny puppet and a picture card. Use different-colored markers to write the onset and the rime of the word for the picture on the chart paper. Invite the class to chant

"I love to rhyme," said the little bunny.
"Rhyming words sound, oh, so funny.
Here is a picture for you to see.
Do you have some rhyming words just for me?"

Invite children to name words that rhyme with the word on the chart paper. Use the same two colors to write the onsets and rimes of the rhyming words children name. Invite children to read aloud the list of words, and encourage them to discuss the spelling pattern that appears in all of the words. Choose a new picture card, and repeat the activity.

BUILDING BINGO BOARDS

Copy and cut apart a set of picture cards, and place them in a container. Write the letters *b, h, m, n, p, r, s,* and *t* on the chalkboard. Give each child some counters and a Bingo reproducible, and invite children to write each letter from the board, in any order, in a separate box on their paper. Draw a picture card, show it to the class, and invite them to say the name of the picture. Tell children to place a counter on the letter that represents the first sound of the word. Repeat the process until a child places three markers in a horizontal, vertical, or diagonal row. Invite children to clear their card, and repeat the activity.

Materials

- ✓ picture cards (82–85)
- ✓ Bingo reproducible (page 92)
- ✓ scissors
- ✓ container
- ✓ counters (e.g., dried beans, pennies)

Concepts

- Letter identification
- Letter formation
- Phonemic awareness

Extensions

- Write the names of eight picture cards on a piece of chart paper. Invite children to write the words in any order in separate boxes on the Bingo reproducible, and repeat the activity.
- Have children write or draw numbers, shapes, colors, or names of animals in separate boxes on the Bingo reproducible, and make a matching set of picture or word cards for use in the activity.

Writing 53

PICTURE THIS!

Materials
- camera/film
- tape
- drawing paper
- bookbinding materials

Concepts
- Critical thinking
- Descriptive language
- Sentence formation
- Letter formation
- Word formation

Extensions
- Make a second set of photographs. Hold up a photograph (e.g., the class library). Have children go to the place they see in the photograph to find the next picture (have a picture of another place waiting for them). Have children follow the trail of photos to a "treasure box" that holds a special treat for them.
- Take photographs of individual children, and have them dictate to you or write a sentence or two about themselves. Bind together the pages, and title the book *Meet Our Class*.

In advance, take photographs of familiar places in and around your school, and have the pictures developed. Give one photograph to each child. Invite children to tape their photograph to a piece of drawing paper and dictate to you or write sentences that describe what they see. Have them read their sentences to the class. Bind together the pages, and title the book *This Is Our School*. Place it in the class or school library.

I play on the swings after lunch.

Enrique

Writing

THIS IS THE PLACE

Cut out several large squares from butcher paper. Invite children to name places they visit in their community, such as the library, the post office, or the grocery store. Write across the top of a square the name of one of these places, such as the fire department, and ask children to help you write sentences about this place at the bottom of the square. For example, children could say *The people who work here wear hats and boots*, *They sleep here at night*, and *They drive big trucks with ladders*. Repeat the process with different paper squares and other places in the community, and invite children to illustrate the pages. Bind the illustrated pages between two blank squares. Title the book *Our Community*, and place it in the class or school library.

Materials

- ✓ scissors
- ✓ butcher paper
- ✓ crayons or markers
- ✓ bookbinding materials

Concepts

- Critical thinking
- Oral language
- Descriptive language
- Sentence formation
- Art

Extensions

- Invite children to color a copy of the House reproducible (page 89) so that it resembles their home. Ask children to dictate to you or write on the back of the paper a sentence or two about their home.

- Write *A _____ is a house for a _____.* on the back of the House reproducible, and write *But a house is a house for me.* on the front side, below the house. Read aloud *A House Is a House for Me* by Mary Ann Hoberman (Viking). Have children complete the first sentence frame on the revised reproducible with a pair of words from the story and illustrate the sentence. Invite children to draw a picture of themselves in the house on the front side.

Writing 55

Materials

- ✓ Bowl reproducible (page 88)
- ✓ crayons or markers
- ✓ magazines
- ✓ scissors
- ✓ glue
- ✓ construction paper
- ✓ bookbinding materials

Concepts

- Critical thinking
- Descriptive language
- Letter formation
- Word formation
- Sentence formation

Extensions

- Read aloud *Growing Vegetable Soup* by Lois Ehlert (Harcourt Brace Jovanovich), and have children draw pictures of vegetables from the story on the Bowl reproducible. Bind together the pages, and title the book *Eating Vegetable Soup*.
- Invite children to color the Bowl reproducible and glue pasta, rice, and dried beans and other vegetables to it. Mount children's work on construction paper, and display their work on a board or wall under the title *What's Cooking?*

SOUP'S ON!

Give each child a Bowl reproducible to color. Invite children to look through magazines and cut out pictures of vegetables. Ask each child to choose one vegetable picture and glue it to his or her bowl. Invite children to think of a sentence that describes their vegetable, such as *This is a red tomato*, and dictate it to you or write it along the bottom of their paper. Glue children's work on pieces of construction paper, bind together the pages, and title the book *Soup's On!* Place the book in the class library.

Writing

WHAT'S IN THE BOX?

Choose holiday (e.g., birthday or Christmas) or thematic (e.g., fish or bug) wrapping paper, and find objects that are related to it (e.g., hat, streamers, and balloons for a birthday). Place the objects in a box, and wrap it with the coordinating paper. Invite children to sit in a circle, and show them the box. Ask children to describe what they see on the wrapping paper and guess the name of the holiday or theme and what might be in the box. Then, say

Knock, knock. What's in the box?
It's all about birthdays. What could it be?
Let's open it up and describe what we see!

Unwrap the box, and invite individual children to take the objects out one at a time and describe them for the class. Give each child a piece of drawing paper. Have children write or draw about the object they like best. Invite them to share their work with the class.

Materials
- wrapping paper
- objects that relate to the pictures on the wrapping paper
- box
- tape
- drawing paper
- crayons or markers

Concepts
- Oral language
- Descriptive language
- Classification
- Critical thinking
- Word formation
- Sentence formation
- Art

Extension
- Celebrate by reading a story and having children eat a snack that coordinates with your holiday or theme.

Writing

Materials

- ✓ Opposites Picture Cards (page 93)
- ✓ Mouse reproducible (page 90)
- ✓ crayons or markers
- ✓ scissors

Concepts

- Compare and contrast
- Critical thinking
- Letter formation
- Word formation
- Art
- Oral reading

Extensions

- Give each child a Mouse reproducible to color. Invite children to cut out their mouse and carry it around the room as they search for a mouse with the matching color.
- Read aloud a version of *Town Mouse, Country Mouse*. Decorate mice cut from the Mouse reproducible to look like the town mouse and the country mouse, and tape them to opposite sides of a piece of chart paper. Invite children to name things that are different about the two mice (e.g., where they live and how they dress), and write their ideas below the mice. Or, attach the mice cutouts to craft sticks, and invite children to use the puppets to retell the story.

TWO OF A KIND, BUT NOT OF LIKE MIND

Copy, color, and cut apart the Opposites Picture Cards. Make a copy of the Mouse reproducible, and write below the mouse the frame *The _____ mouse likes _____*. Display a pair of cards, and ask children to explain what makes them different. Give each child a double-sided copy of the revised Mouse reproducible. Ask children to color each mouse a different color. Help children write on the first blank line of each sentence frame the colors of their mice. Have children choose a pair of opposites, such as up and down, and write on the second blank line of each sentence these words. Tell children to draw pictures about the opposite words beside the corresponding mice. Invite children to read aloud their sentences to the class.

The <u>blue</u> mouse likes <u>day</u>.

Marcus

58 Writing

DOWN BY THE PARK

Give each child a Down by the Park reproducible. Name nouns with familiar rimes, such as *bat*, *block*, or *cup*, and invite children to name another noun that rhymes with each word. Write the pairs of rhyming words on a piece of chart paper, and display it. Invite children to choose words to complete the frames on the reproducible so that they rhyme. For example, a child could write

Down by the park where the flowers grow,
Back to my school I dare not go.
For if I do my teacher will remark,
"Have you ever seen a <u>bat</u>
<u>Wearing a hat</u> down by the park?"

Invite children to dictate words to you or write their own words and then illustrate their work. Bind together children's papers, and title the book *Down by the Park*.

bat	hat
glue	shoe
goat	coat
pie	tie
hen	pen

Materials

✓ Down by the Park reproducible (page 94)
✓ chart paper
✓ crayons or markers
✓ bookbinding materials

Concepts

- Parts of speech
- Rhyming words
- Letter formation
- Word formation
- Art

Extensions

- Read aloud *Down by the Bay* by Raffi (Crown). Ask children to identify the pairs of rhyming words in the book.
- Invite children to change the setting from a school to another place, such as a farm or a pool, and repeat the activity.

Writing

Animal Poetry

Materials
- Animal Poetry reproducible (page 95)
- tape
- chart stand
- crayons or markers

Concepts
- Shared writing
- Art
- Science

Extensions
- Invite the class to change a few of the words in the poem frame to write about a mode of transportation. For example,

  One, two, a <u>train</u> sees you.
  Three, four, <u>watch it chug</u> some more.
  Five, six, <u>coal</u> is the fuel it picks.
  Seven, eight, its <u>whistle</u> is great!

- Have children cut eye and mouth holes in paper grocery sacks. Invite children to choose an animal from the *Odes to Animals* class display and decorate their grocery sack to look like it. Invite them to wear their mask and read aloud the poem about their animal.

Make several enlarged copies of the Animal Poetry reproducible, and tape one copy to a chart stand. Invite children to name an animal (e.g., a penguin), and write its name on the first blank line of the poem. Ask them to name something they like to watch or hear the animal do (e.g., watch it dive), and complete the second line. Ask children what this animal eats (e.g., fish), and complete the third line. Invite children to name something unique about this animal (e.g., its waddle), and complete the fourth line. Repeat the activity with another enlarged copy of the poem and a new animal. Invite children to illustrate the poem pages with pictures of the animals, and display the pages on a board or wall under the title *Odes to Animals*.

Animal Poetry

One, two, a <u>lion</u> sees you.
Three, four, <u>hear it roar</u> some more.
Five, six, <u>meat</u> is the food it picks.
Seven, eight, its <u>mane</u> is great!

60 Writing

BIRTHDAY GREETINGS

Early in the school year, invite children to make greeting cards to present to their classmates as birthday gifts. Give each child a Greeting Card reproducible and the name of a classmate. Invite children to dictate to you or write a special message for their card. Tell them to sign their card with *(child's name) and The students in Room ___*. Have children cut out the card and color it. Collect the cards, and invite children to present their card on behalf of the class on their classmate's birthday.

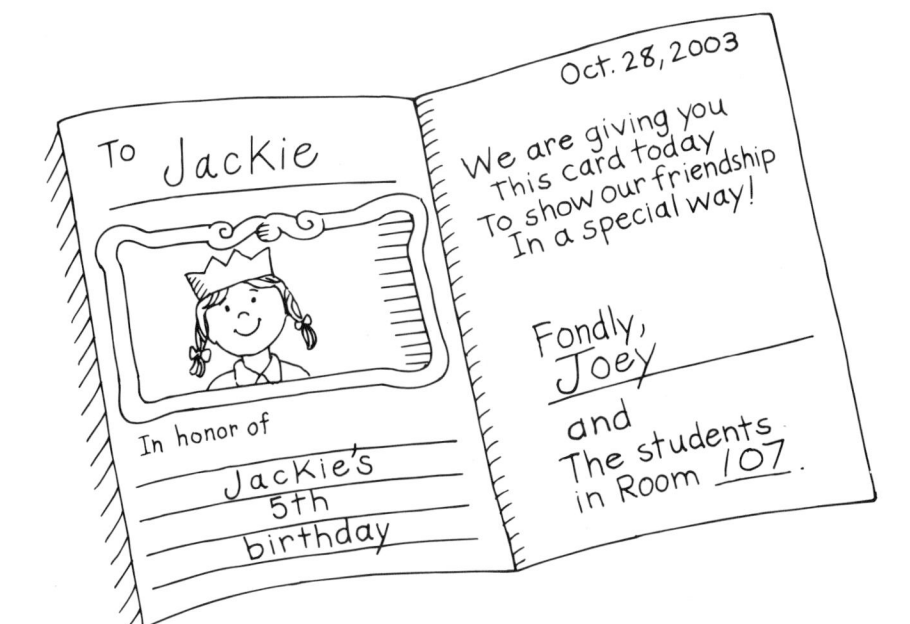

Materials

- Greeting Card reproducible (page 96)
- scissors
- crayons or markers

Concepts

- Letter formation
- Word formation
- Sentence formation
- Social interaction
- Self-esteem

Extensions

- Mark children's birthdays on a large calendar. Occasionally, invite children to count the number of days until their birthday arrives.
- Use the Greeting Card reproducible to create cards for other special events, such as thank-you notes to parent volunteers or holiday cards for family and friends.

Writing 61

Bugs

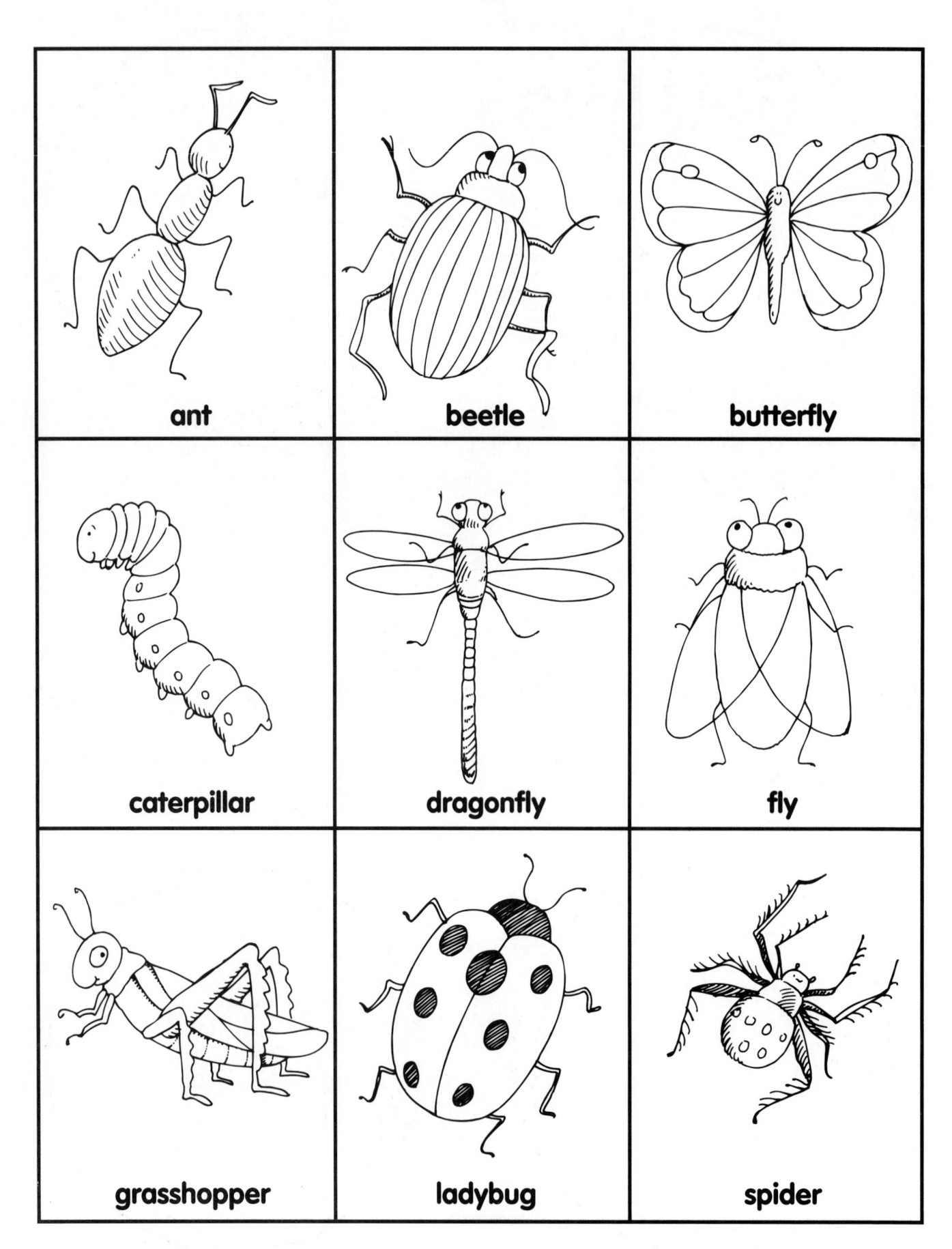

ant	beetle	butterfly
caterpillar	dragonfly	fly
grasshopper	ladybug	spider

Cookies

Shapes in Our World

Name _____   Date _____

Letter Cards

a	b	c
d	e	f
g	h	i

Letter Cards

j	k	l
m	n	o
p	q	r

Letter Cards

s	t	u
v	w	x
y	z	

Number Cards

0	1	2
3	4	5
6	7	8

Number Cards

9	10	11
12	13	14
15	16	17

Fast or Slow Picture Cards

Animal Picture Cards

Stoplight

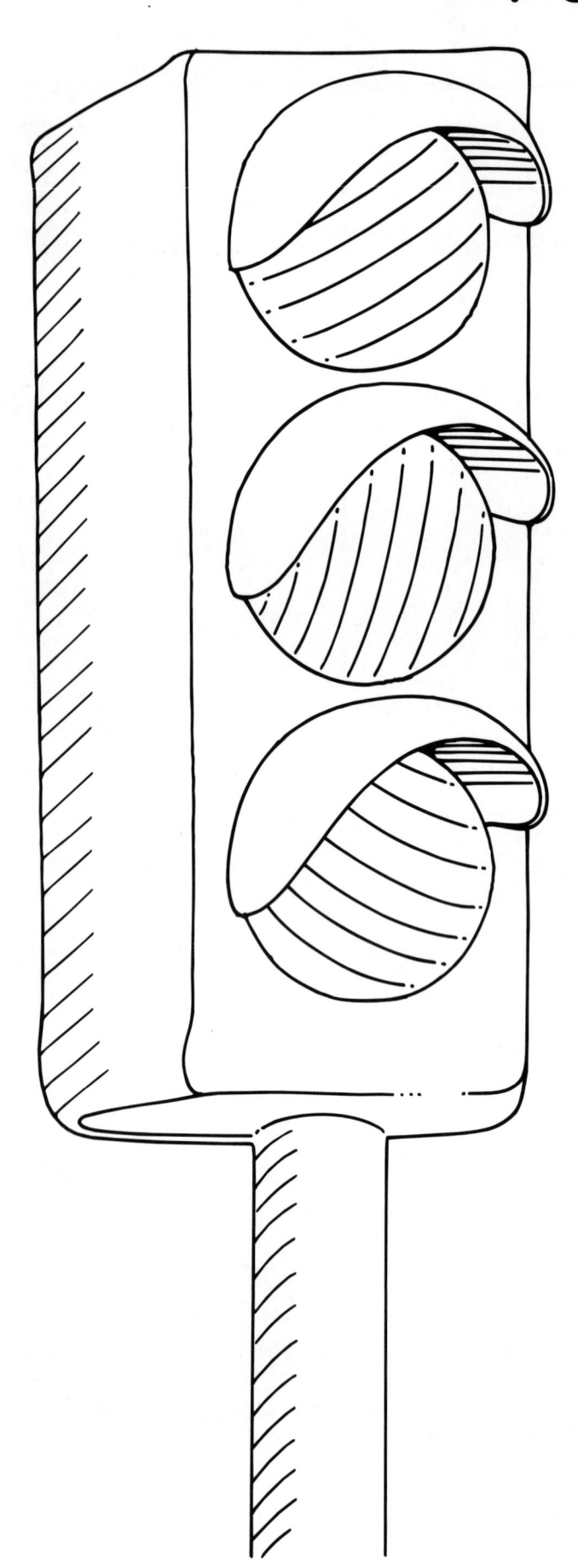

Red means stop.

Yellow means slow.

Green means that

it's time to go.

Start your engines.

Look high and low.

Now grab the wheel.

It's off we go!

Worms

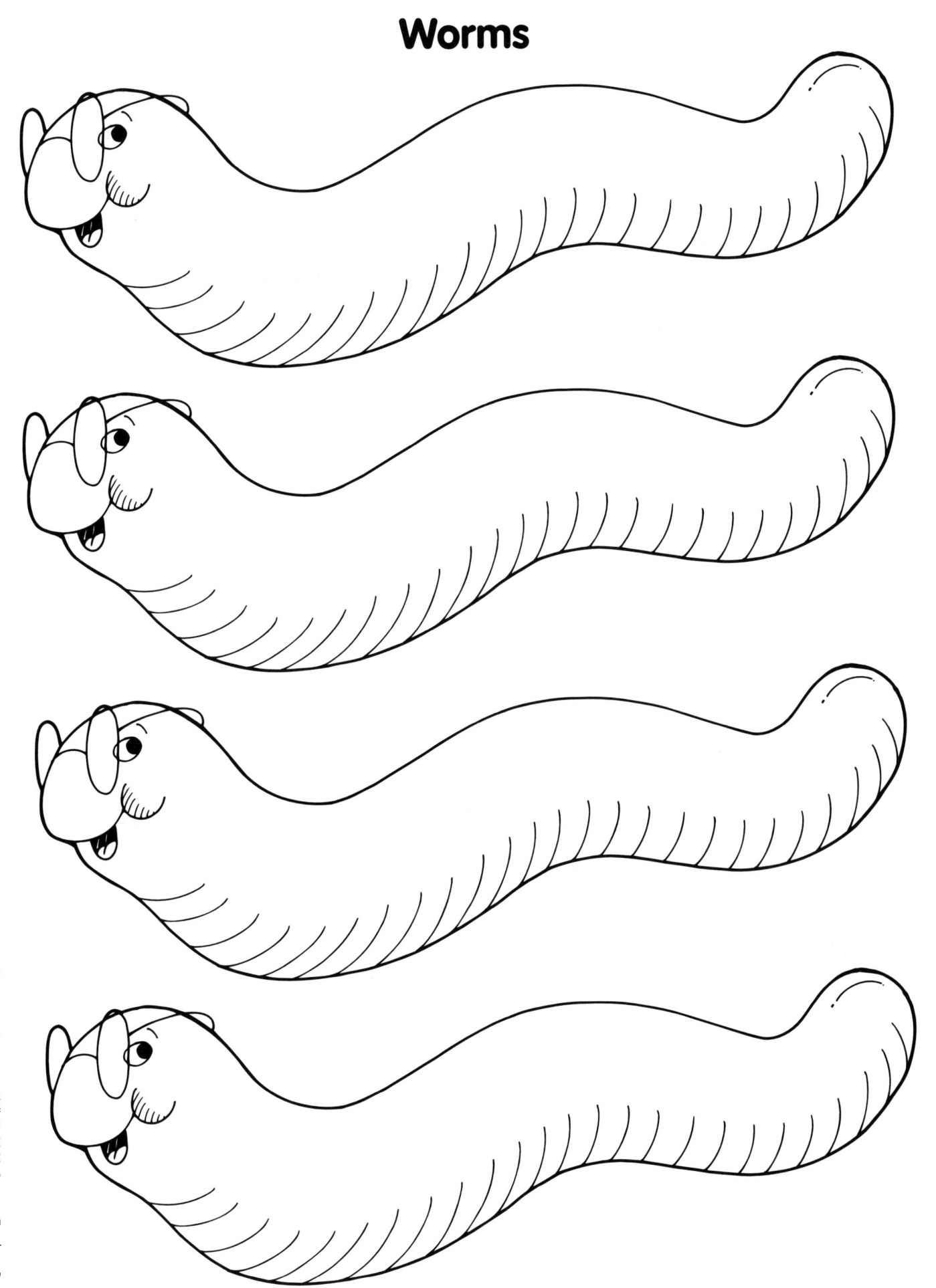

Web

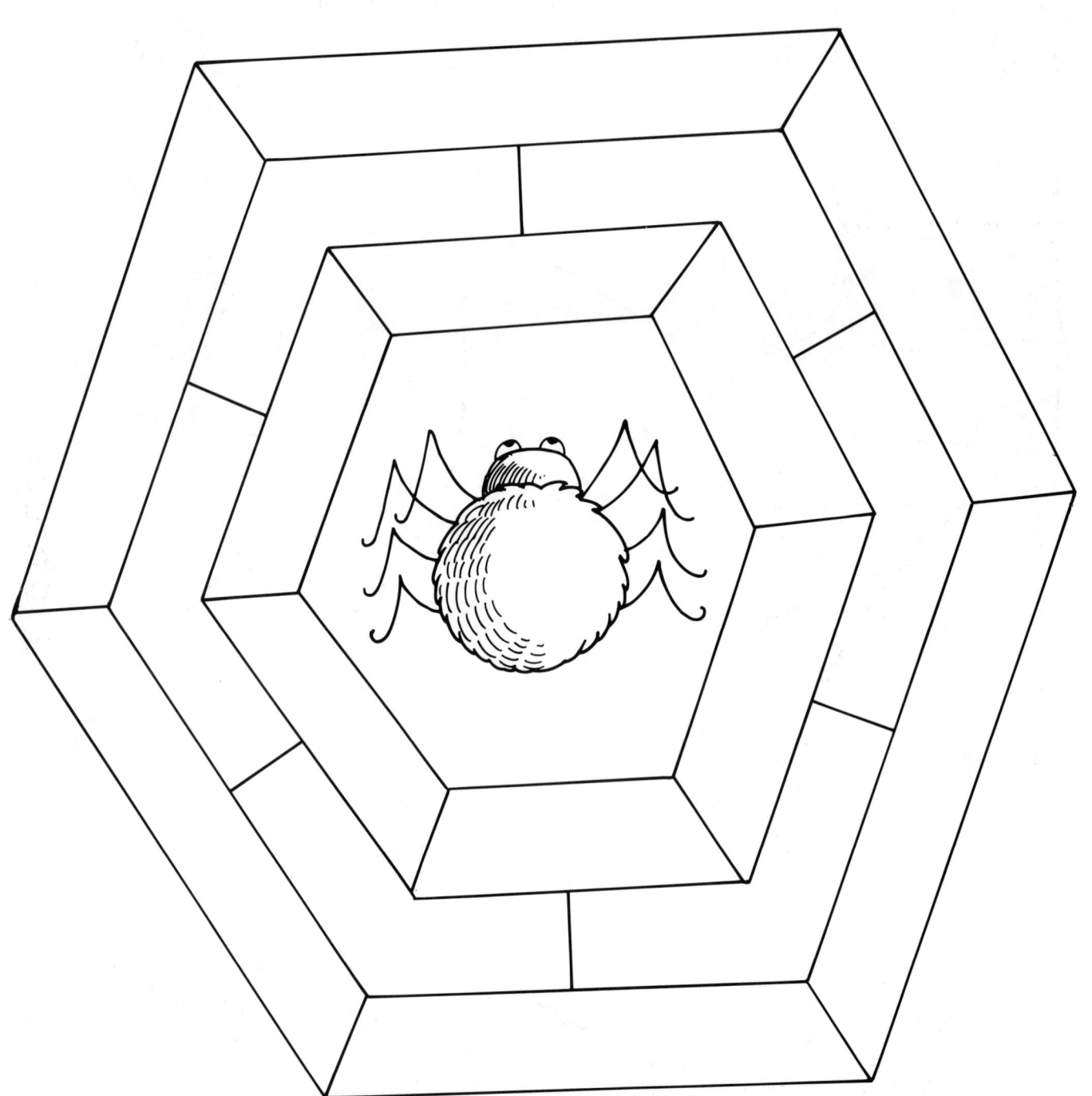

Dinosaur

Coat

Sharing Can Parent Letter

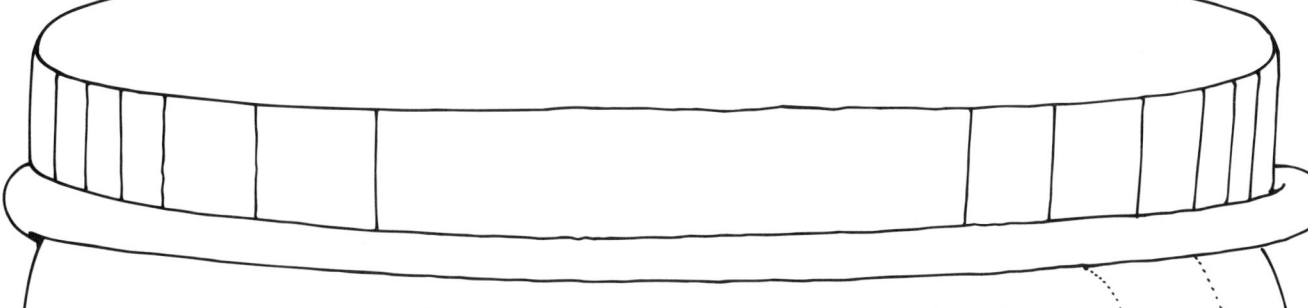

Dear Family,

It is your child's turn to bring something special to share at school. Please do the following things with your child:

1. Help your child choose something special to place in the Sharing Can.
2. Together, think of three ways to describe this object.
3. Write your ideas on a piece of paper, and place the paper in the can.
4. Return the can to school tomorrow.

Have fun!

Holiday Picture Cards

New Year's Day	Martin Luther King Jr.'s Birthday	Groundhog Day
Valentine's Day	Presidents' Day	St. Patrick's Day
Easter	Fourth of July	Halloween
Thanksgiving	Christmas	Chanukah

Nursery Rhyme Picture Cards

Mask

Vegetable Picture Cards

bean	broccoli	carrot
corn	cucumber	lettuce
onion	peas	potato
pumpkin	squash	tomato

Picture Cards

Picture Cards

Picture Cards

Picture Cards

Fish

Frog

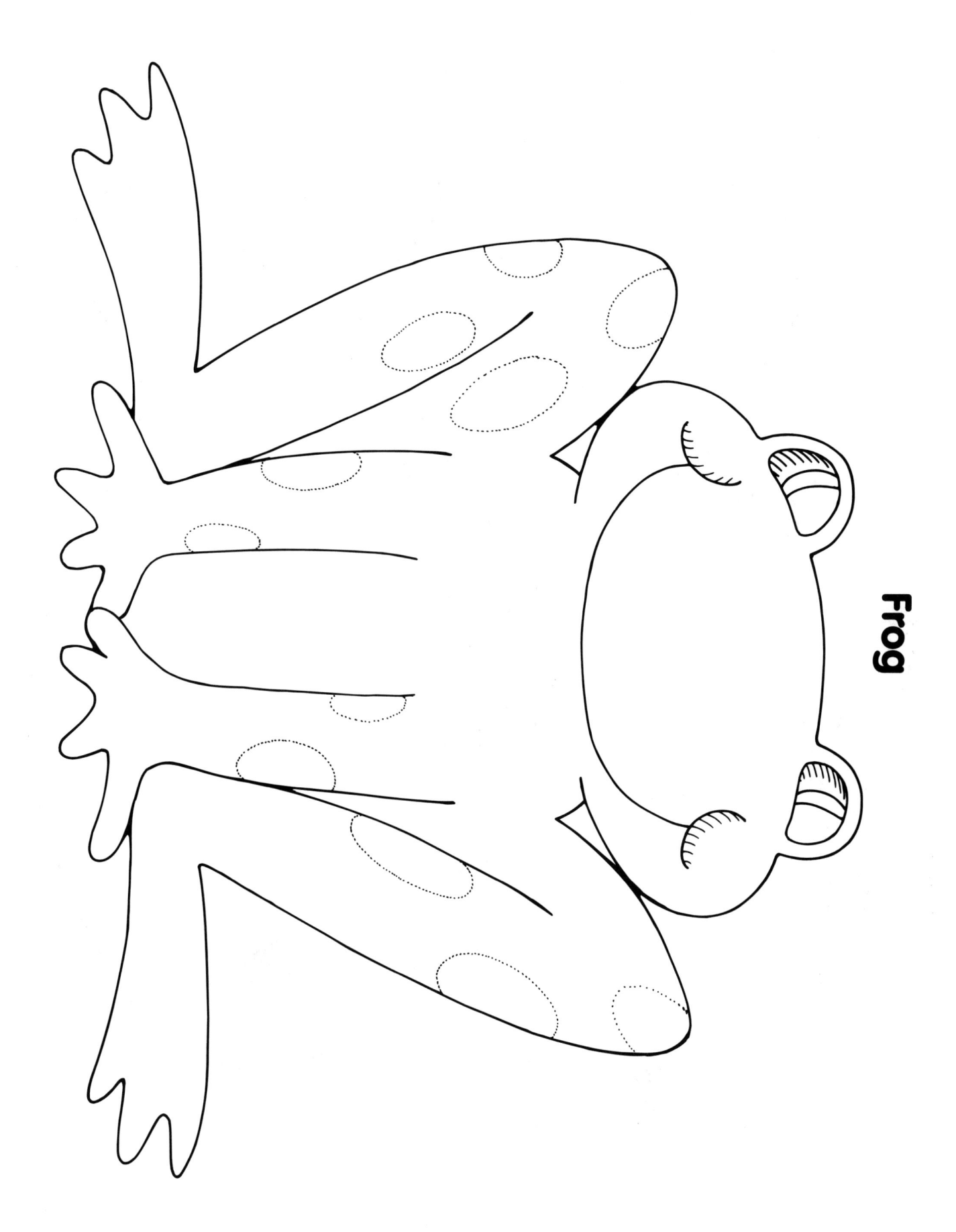

Bowl

House

Mouse

Bunny

Bingo

	Free Space	

Opposites Picture Cards

hot	cold	up
down	day	night
front	back	in
out	happy	sad

Down by the Park

Name _____ Date _____

Down by the park where the flowers grow,
Back to my school I dare not go.
For if I do my teacher will remark,
"Have you ever seen a _____
_____
down by the park?"

Animal Poetry

One, two, a _____ sees you.

Three, four, _____ some more.

Five, six, _____ is the food it picks.

Seven, eight, its _____ is great!

Greeting Card

We are giving you
This card today
To show our friendship
In a special way!

Fondly,

_____
and
The students
in Room ____.

To _____

In honor of
_____